Seas and Weather

By Linda Bruce

Northern hemisphere

Spring	March	April	May
Summer	June	July	August
Autumn	September	October	November
Winter	December	January	February

Southern hemisphere

Spring	September	October	November
Summer	December	January	February
Autumn	March	April	May
Winter	June	July	August

Contents

Introduction	4
Why There Are Seasons	6
Summer	8
How to Press Flowers	10
Autumn	12
Deciduous or Evergreen?	14
Migration	16
Winter	18
Hibernation	20
The Black Bear	21
Spring	22
Questions	24
Glossary	24
Index	25

John Brown University
Library
Siloam Springs, AR

Introduction

As the year passes, the seasons change. In most places, there are four seasons: summer, autumn, winter, and spring.

During summer, we can play outside in the hot weather.

In autumn, the weather is cooler. The leaves on many trees change color and fall to the ground.

In some places, it snows in winter.
The weather is very cold.

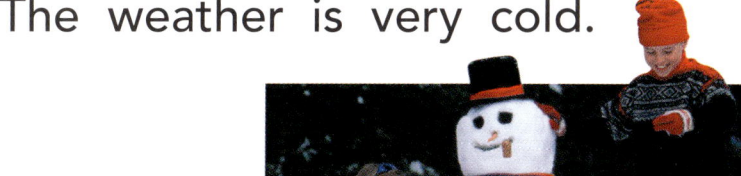

In spring,
the weather gets warmer again.
Plants grow new flowers and leaves.

There are changes all around us
during the year.

Why there are seasons

The Earth moves around the Sun. As it moves, the seasons change.

Summer: long, hot days (and short nights)

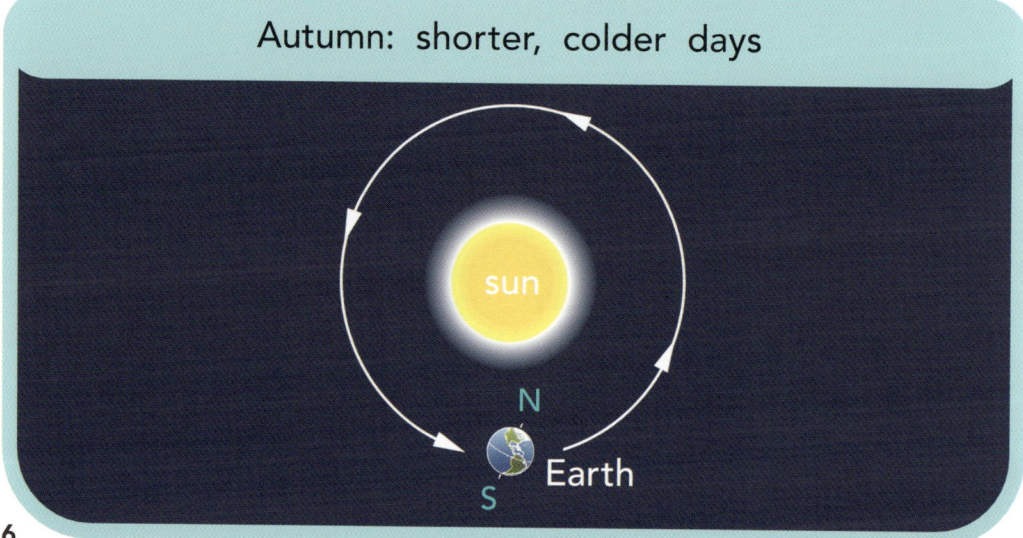

Autumn: shorter, colder days

Did you know?

Each season lasts about three months.

Key
N = North
S = South

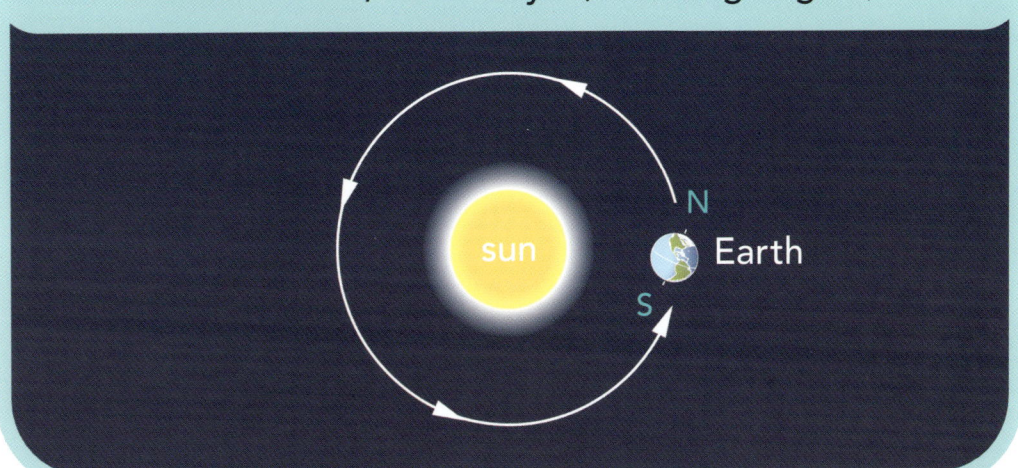

Winter: short, cold days (and long nights)

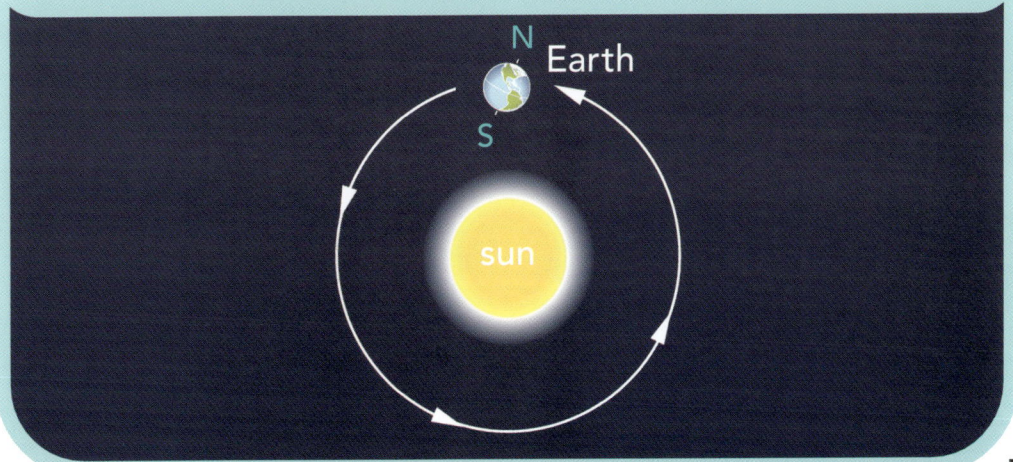

Spring: longer, warmer days

Summer

In summer, the weather is hot and the days are long.

All the trees have leaves, and fruit is growing bigger.

Some fruit is ready for picking.

Birds have lots of insects to eat.

To stay cool,
people wear light clothes.
Some people go for a swim.

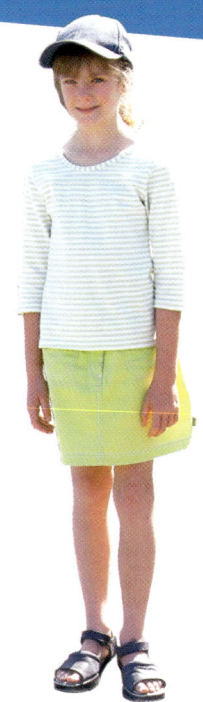

Others sit under trees, in the shade.

How to Press Flowers

1. Cut some flowers from the garden.

2. Find a heavy book and some paper.

3. Place the flowers between the paper.

4. Put the book on top of the paper. Leave it there for about two weeks.

In summer, it is fun to press flowers.

Autumn

In autumn, the days are shorter and cooler.

It is time to pick different kinds of fruit.

In the sky, there are many birds flying to warmer places.
They need to find more food.

Some animals are finding places to sleep for the winter.
Others are moving from high in the mountains to hills lower down, where it is warmer.

Deciduous or Evergreen?

Some trees lose their leaves in autumn. These trees are called deciduous trees. At first, the leaves change color and die. Then they fall to the ground.

DID YOU KNOW?

Fall and autumn are different names for the same season.

Other trees grow new leaves all year round. These trees are called evergreen trees.

Migration

Many birds, and some animals, move to warmer places when winter is coming. This is called migration.

hummingbird

This tiny bird flies a long way to find a warmer place for winter.

Fruit bats also fly
to warmer places.
They need to find fruit to eat
during winter.

DID YOU KNOW?

When winter is near,
whales swim to warmer waters
to have their babies.

Winter

In winter, the days are short,
and the nights are long.
This is the coldest time of the year.

Often, the sky is full
of dark, gray rain clouds.

People need to wear heavy clothes to stay warm.

In some places, it is so cold that it snows.

DID YOU KNOW?

Snow is tiny drops of ice that are made in clouds when it is very cold.

Rivers and ponds are covered in ice.

Hibernation

Some animals go to sleep for the winter. They find safe places out of the cold. This is called hibernation.

As the weather gets warmer in spring, the animals wake up and look for food.

The Black Bear

The black bear hibernates for many months.

The bear finds a cave, or uses a hollow log for its winter home.

When the snow melts, the bear comes out of its shelter into the warm spring weather.

Spring

In spring, the sun shines more.
The days grow longer and warmer.

The snow melts and flows into rivers.

Trees have blossoms and tiny green leaves.

Birds build nests
and sit on their eggs.

Baby animals are everywhere.

Soon it will be summer.
A whole year has nearly passed.

Questions

1. How long does each season last?
2. What are the two names for the same season?
3. What do whales do when winter is near?
4. What is snow, and where is it made?

Glossary

blossom   a small flower, most often found on fruit trees

hibernation sleeping in a safe place for the whole winter

hollow   having a hole or space in the middle

migration   going a long way to live in another place

shelter   a safe place to stay to get away from bad weather